Wild and tame

donkey

tame cat

dog

pig

sheep

These animals are tame.

wild ass

wild cat

wolf

boar

mouflon

These animals are wild.

This book is about wild animals.
They have to find their own food.
People help tame animals find food.

1

Woodlands

These animals live in woodlands in cool countries.
Sometimes they live in fields near the woods.

2

red squirrels

fox

stoat

adder

mole

rabbit

harvest mice

A badger's home is called a set. Badgers make tunnels in the earth for their home. They stay in the tunnels by day and come out to feed at night.

A beaver's home is called a lodge. Beavers build lodges in shallow streams and rivers. The lodge is made with branches and logs. The way into the lodge is under the water.

Hedgehogs live in long grass in the woodlands and fields. They only come out at night for food. Hedgehogs are covered in spikes, called spines. When they are frightened they curl into a ball with the spines sticking out.

Most animals in this picture have four feet.
Try to find the two that have no feet at all.

3

Forest animals

brown bear
boar
wolf
wild cat
badger
pine marten

These animals live in the forest.
Most of them are hunters.
They can all move quickly.

lynx

red squirrel

pole cat

Wolves hunt in packs at the edge of the forest. They often work together to catch their prey. Can you see how they do it?

Wolverines live in North America and Europe. They hunt small animals.

Bears eat berries and honey as well as meat. They sometimes catch fish.

Only a few bison are left in Europe now. Some also live in North America, where they are called buffalo.

Many forest animals have sharp claws which help them climb trees.
They all have coats of hair or fur.

Mountains

In summer pikas collect grass and dry it to make hay. They store this hay to eat in winter.

Lemmings live in Norway. Sometimes they travel a long way. Many drown in the rivers they have to cross.

ibex
yak
Himalayan black bear
Himalayan brown bear
goral
Himalayan marten
mountain hare
clouded leopard

The clouded leopard is very rare. It lives high up in the mountains. Can you find a member of the goat family in the picture?

puma

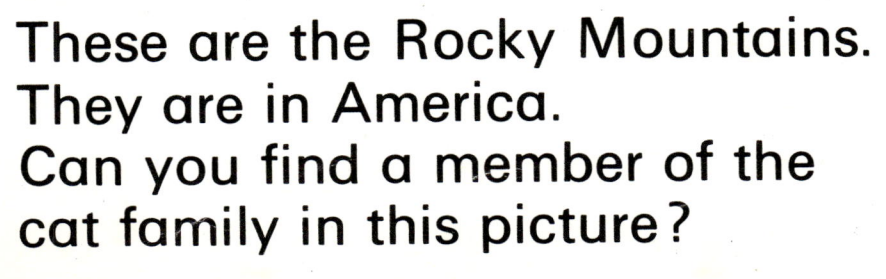

bighorn sheep

grizzly bear

beaver

marmot

raccoon

chipmunks

ibex

Rocky Mountain goat

domestic ram

angora goat

These mountain sheep and goats come from different parts of the world. They are all good at climbing, and jumping from rock to rock.

These are the Rocky Mountains.
They are in America.
Can you find a member of the
cat family in this picture?

7

Desert animals

Some desert animals have large ears. These help to keep them cool.

The naked mole rat lives underground. It has no hair.

The golden mole is blind. Its eyes are covered with skin. It lives underground.

springbok

ostriches

wild asses

desert antelope

caracal lynx

gerbils

fennec fox

There is very little water in deserts. Some desert animals hardly ever drink.

8

puma
bobcats
kit fox
coyote
jackrabbit
white footed mice
kangaroo rats

The bactrian camel has two humps. Some still live wild in the Gobi desert in Asia.

Camels were taken to Australia to work there. A few escaped and now live wild. Kangaroos also live wild in Australia.

A camel which has had no water gets very thin. It gets fatter again when it has had a drink.

The big animals hunt the smaller ones. Can you see how the mice and rats keep safe?

9

Grasslands (1)

The hot African grasslands were once full of animals. Hunters killed too many of them.

There are few places to hide in on the grasslands. The animals must run fast to escape from their enemies.

Some grasslands are now called parks.
Animals are safe in the parks.
People must not hunt them there.

Grasslands (2)

Prairie dogs are ground squirrels. They live together in large groups. These groups are called towns. Sometimes thousands of prairie dogs live in one town. They like to visit one another's burrows.

The grasslands of North America are cooler than the African grasslands. Different kinds of animals live there.

12

Ratels live in the grasslands of Asia and Africa. They like to eat honey. They are often called honey badgers. A bird called a honeyguide sometimes leads the ratel to a bees' nest. The bird can eat the honey the ratel leaves.

The mongoose is good at killing snakes that live in the grasslands. It jumps about too fast for the snake to catch it.

The Indian rhino lives in the hot grasslands. It is becoming very rare. There are some in zoos, but not many are left wild in India.

These animals live in the grasslands of South America. Which animal has scales?

13

Jungles (1)

Chimpanzees live in trees. They live together in tribes.

Baby chimpanzees stay with their mothers for a long time.

Chimpanzees are not grown up until they are eight years old.

Chimpanzees can laugh and smile like people.

colobus monkeys

fruit eating bat

flying squirrel

elephants

porcupine

crocodile

mandrill

chameleon

This jungle is in Africa.
It is hot and wet here.
The animals live among the trees.

14

Many jungle animals hide in the trees
to keep safe from their enemies.
How many can you find?

Jungles (2)

This jungle is in Asia. Animals come to drink at the pool.

16

These animals live
in the jungles of South America.
Jaguars and huge snakes live there.

17

In cold places

polar bears
seals
moose
Arctic fox
lemmings
ermine

These animals live in cold countries.
Some sleep through the winter.
Some must look for food in the snow.

musk oxen

walrus

reindeer

Arctic hares

ground squirrels

stoat ermine

fox

snowshoe rabbit

Some animals in cold lands have white coats in winter. These do not show up in the snow. Look at them in their summer and winter coats. A stoat in its white coat is called ermine.

Seals and penguins live in the Antarctic. Very few other animals live there.

Polar bears hunt and catch fish.
Wolves and foxes catch small animals.
Reindeer dig in the snow for moss.

19

Australia

Before a kangaroo has a baby she cleans her pouch.

When it is born the baby kangaroo is very tiny. It crawls into its mother's pouch.

The mother kangaroo gives milk to the baby in her pouch.

When the baby gets bigger it looks out of the pouch. When it is about eight months old it stays out of the pouch and hops about like its mother.

dingos

red kangaroo

rat kangaroo

nail tail wallaby

swamp rat

enchinida

rabbit

quokka

These animals live in Australia. Most of the mother animals carry their babies in pouches.

Animals with pouches
are called marsupials.
Kangaroos are marsupials.

21

Rare animals

giant panda

musk ox

aye-aye

koala

tiger

These animals are very rare.
Most of them have been killed
by men for their fur or their meat.

cheetah

polar bear

orang utan

Indian rhinoceros

Some animals die out
when men chop down forests.
They have nowhere to live.

23

Families

The cat family

- lynx
- wild cat
- cheetah
- tiger
- lion
- leopard
- jaguar

The dog family

- wolf
- coyote
- jackal
- fennec fox
- fox
- Cape hunting dog
- dingo

Here are some families of animals. Can you see how the members of a family are alike?

The panda family

red panda
coati
olingo
giant panda
kinkajou
cacomistle
raccoon

The ape family

chimpanzee
gibbon
orang utan
gorilla

person

Which family do tigers belong to?
Which animals are most like people?
Which is the raccoon's family?

25

Long ago

mammoth

giant ground sloth

giant armadillo

These animals lived long ago.
They have all died out now.
Nobody is sure what they looked like.

26

Sometimes people find their bones in rocks.
Scientists guess what they looked like.

27

How animals live

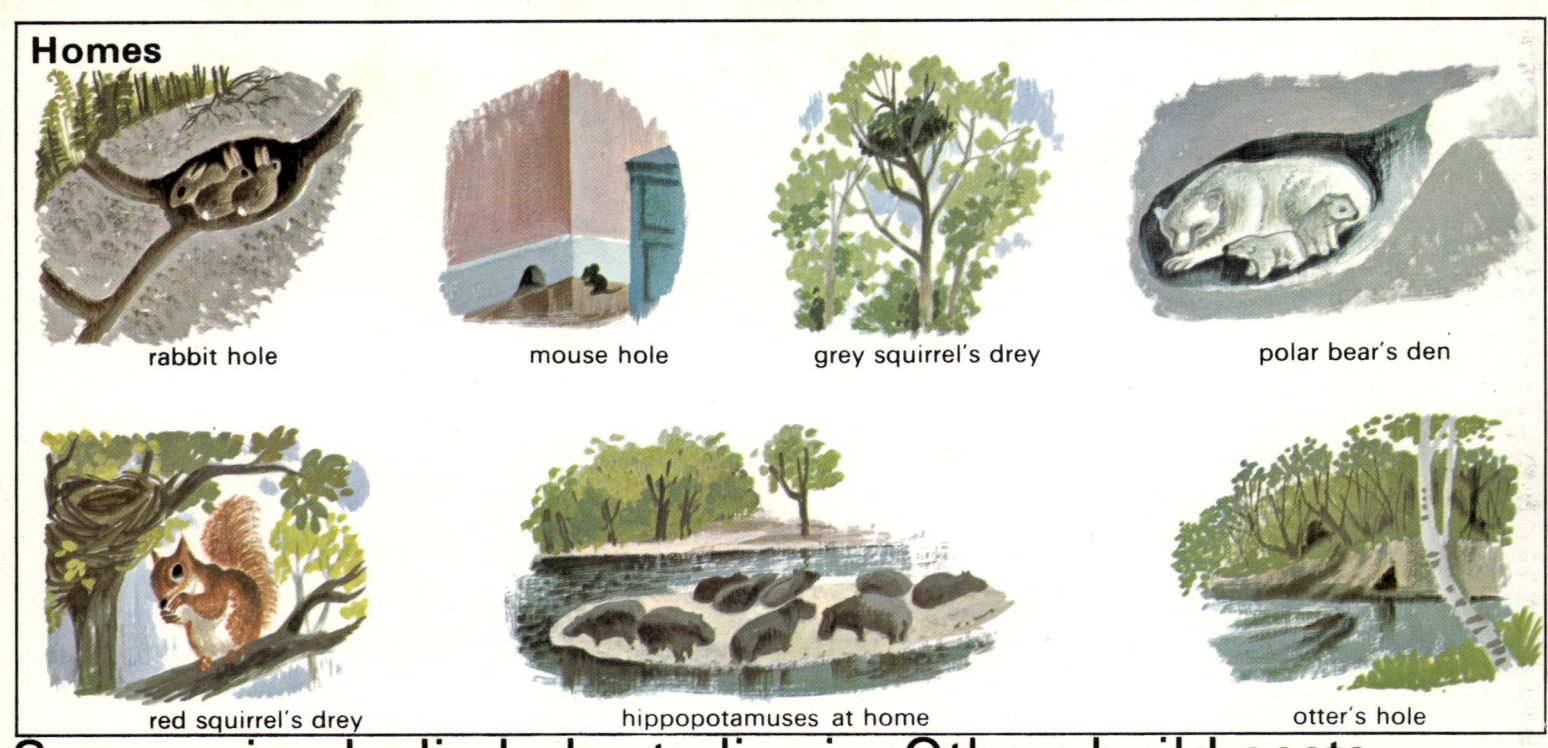

Homes

rabbit hole | mouse hole | grey squirrel's drey | polar bear's den

red squirrel's drey | hippopotamuses at home | otter's hole

Some animals dig holes to live in. Others build nests. Some do not build homes. They live in the open air.

Food

lion | grey squirrel | rabbit | otter

hedgehog | anteater | mouse | koala

Some animals eat meat. Some eat grass or seeds. The anteater only eats ants.